Part of the "NEARBY" series of books.

THE FARM

Part of the "Nearby" series of books.

BY: DA BUTLER

On a Saturday afternoon, brothers Arthur and Andy were playing a game in the kitchen. Their mother came in and asked, "boys, would you like to go and see a farm today? We can go and pick our own vegetables, go for a wagon ride and look for animals."

Arthur and Andy had never been to a farm before. They had talked about farms in school and their teacher said that a lot of their fruits, vegetables and milk comes from local farms.

After a short car ride, Arthur and Andy hopped out of the car and were amazed at how big the farm was. Farmer Jake greeted them and welcomed them to his farm.

Farmer Jake said that his farm grows carrots and potatoes. He explained that carrots and potatoes are root vegetables. That means that they both grow underground. They have many vitamins and minerals that help our bodies to grow and stay healthy.

"Do you boys like french fries? French fries are made from potatoes!"

"We love french fries," replied the boys.

After they looked around the field and pulled up some carrots and potatoes they all headed back to the barn to wash up.

Farmer Jake led Arthur, Andy and their mom to see the cows. They watched as all of the cows were hooked up to the milking machines. The milk was pumped and flowed through a pipe to a large tank where it is stored and kept until it can be transported by truck to be processed and ready to drink.

"That was so cool," said Arthur.

"I want to be a farmer when I grow up!" said Andy.

Farmer Jake told the boys that now they can go on a fun hayride around the farm. They hopped on the wagon and Farmer Jake drove the tractor around the farm. He pointed out the fields, the pond and at the far end of the property there was a small apple orchard.

"Can we pick apples, Farmer Jake?" asked Arthur.

"The apples won't be ready for a few more weeks. They are usually ready to start picking by the end of the summer. You can come back then and pick all of the apples you want!"

The wagon arrived back at the barn and the boys jumped off.

"That was really fun," said Andy.

"Yes, thank you," echoed Arthur.

The boys and their mom said goodbye to Farmer Jake and they headed back home. All the way home the boys talked about picking vegetables, watching the cows being milked and having so much fun on the wagon ride. They can't wait to come back and pick apples!

More titles in the NEARBY series:

The Backyard
The Fire Station
The Library

Other DA BUTLER titles:
My Glasses
Freckles!
My Daddy
Kindness
Forever Friend
The New Baby

www.ingramcontent.com/pod-product-compliance
Lightning Source LLC
Chambersburg PA
CBHW041403010526
44107CB00015B/1054